FIRST SOLOS

FOR THE
TUBA PLAYER

SELECTED AND ARRANGED FOR TUBA AND PIANO
(INCLUDING SEVEN DUETS FOR TWO TUBAS)

BY **HERBERT WEKSELBLATT**

G. SCHIRMER, Inc.

DISTRIBUTED BY

HAL•LEONARD®
CORPORATION

7777 W. BLUEMOUND RD. P.O. BOX 13819 MILWAUKEE, WI 53213

D. 2897

FOREWORD

Music teachers and tuba players have long felt a need for a collection of solo pieces prepared for the beginning player. Every tuba player who has graduated from the oom-pah style of band music hopes some day to be able to play solos. After mastering this album of music the fledgling soloist will be well on the way to more advanced material.

I have chosen the material keeping in mind the traditional solos that all tuba players will eventually play. The easiest are: *The Battle Hymn of the Republic, When Johnny Comes Marching Home,* and the *Military Songs* . . . all known and sung from childhood. The traditional solos are: *Asleep in the Deep, The Happy Farmer* variations, and *Down in the Deep, Deep Cellar* variations. As an additional challenge, the solo portion of the book ends with the *Carnival of Venice* with two variations adapted from Arban.

An important consideration has been the piano accompaniment. I have tried to realize the most effective accompaniment for the tuba and at the same time make the piano part easily playable.

The duets have been included for the education and enjoyment of the student. Some of them are easy to play and will help him to learn how to consider tonal balance and intonation in his playing. Others are more difficult and will not only challenge technical skill but also his musicianship.

My sincere thanks to Susan Kagan who collaborated with me in the piano realizations needed for this book.

H. W.

CONTENTS

		Piano	Tuba
1.	CIVIL WAR MEDLEY		
	Battle Hymn of the Republic	2	2
	When Johnny Comes Marching Home	3	2
2.	THE HAPPY FARMER. Robert Schumann	4	3
	(Variations from Album for the Young)		
3.	THE WILD HORSEMAN. Robert Schumann	7	4
	(from Album for the Young)		
4.	MILITARY SUITE		
	The Marine's Hymn	8	4
	The Caisson Song	9	4
	Anchors Away	11	5
5.	OXFORD GAVOTTE. Susan Kagan	13	6
6.	IN THE HALL OF THE MOUNTAIN KING. Edvard Grieg	14	6
	(from Peer Gynt)		
7.	ASLEEP IN THE DEEP. H. W. Perrie	18	8
8.	MARCH OF A MARIONETTE. Charles Gounod	20	9
9.	MUSETTE. Johann Sebastian Bach	22	9
10.	GAVOTTE. Jean-Baptiste Lully	23	10
11.	MARCHE. Wolfgang Amadeus Mozart	25	10
	(from Les Petits Riens)		
12.	LA VILLAGEOISE. Philippe Rameau	27	11
13.	COUNTRY DANCE. Ludwig van Beethoven	28	12
14.	HORNPIPE (American Folk Dance)	29	12
15.	FALSTAFF'S DRINKING SONG. Otto Nicolai	31	13
	(from The Merry Wives of Windsor)		
16.	DOWN IN THE DEEP CELLAR. Ludwig Fischer	32	13
17.	THE CARNIVAL OF VENICE (Variations). J. B. Arban	34	14
18.	SEVEN DUETS		15

FIRST SOLOS FOR THE TUBA PLAYER

Selected and Arranged by Herbert Wekselblatt

1. Civil War Medley

When Johnny Comes Marching Home

2. The Happy Farmer

(Variations)

from: Album for the Young

Robert Schumann (1810-1856)

Var. 1

6

3. The Wild Horseman

from: Album for the Young

Robert Schumann

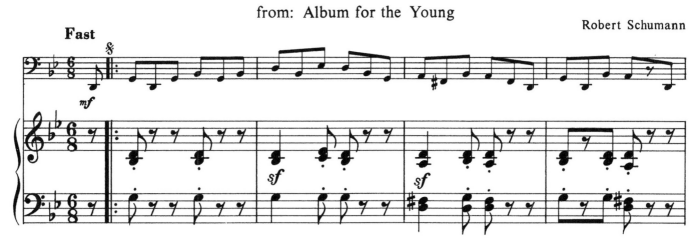

47007

4. Military Suite

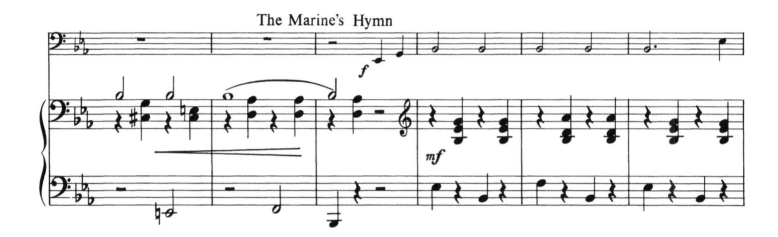

The Marine's Hymn

The Caisson Song

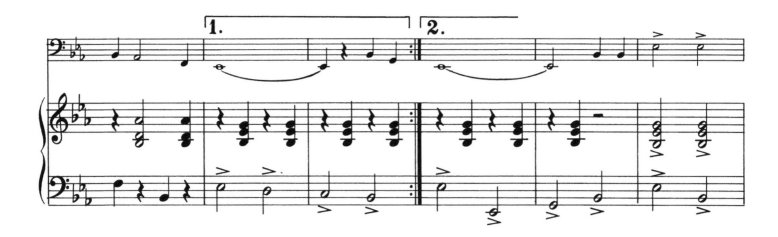

Anchors Aweigh

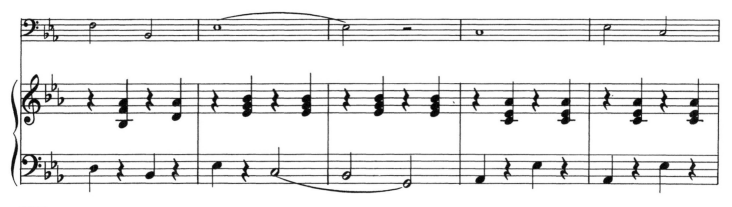

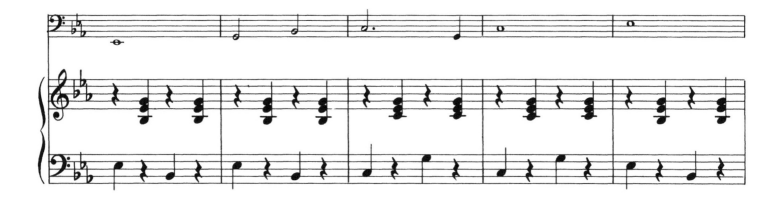

5. Oxford Gavotte

Susan Kagan

6. In the Hall of the Mountain King

from: Peer Gynt

Edvard Grieg (1843-1907)

Slowly at first then faster

47007

FIRST
SOLOS
FOR THE
TUBA
PLAYER

SELECTED AND ARRANGED FOR TUBA AND PIANO
(INCLUDING SEVEN DUETS FOR TWO TUBAS)

BY **HERBERT WEKSELBLATT**

G. SCHIRMER, Inc.

DISTRIBUTED BY
HAL•LEONARD®
CORPORATION
7777 W. BLUEMOUND RD. P.O. BOX 13819 MILWAUKEE, WI 53213

ED. 2897

FOREWORD

Music teachers and tuba players have long felt a need for a collection of solo pieces prepared for the beginning player. Every tuba player who has graduated from the oom-pah style of band music hopes some day to be able to play solos. After mastering this album of music the fledgling soloist will be well on the way to more advanced material.

I have chosen the material keeping in mind the traditional solos that all tuba players will eventually play. The easiest are: *The Battle Hymn of the Republic, When Johnny Comes Marching Home,* and the *Military Songs* . . . all known and sung from childhood. The traditional solos are: *Asleep in the Deep, The Happy Farmer* variations, and *Down in the Deep, Deep Cellar* variations. As an additional challenge, the solo portion of the book ends with the *Carnival of Venice* with two variations adapted from Arban.

An important consideration has been the piano accompaniment. I have tried to realize the most effective accompaniment for the tuba and at the same time make the piano part easily playable.

The duets have been included for the education and enjoyment of the student. Some of them are easy to play and will help him to learn how to consider tonal balance and intonation in his playing. Others are more difficult and will not only challenge technical skill but also his musicianship.

My sincere thanks to Susan Kagan who collaborated with me in the piano realizations needed for this book.

H. W.

CONTENTS

	Piano	Tuba
1. CIVIL WAR MEDLEY		
Battle Hymn of the Republic	2	2
When Johnny Comes Marching Home	3	2
2. THE HAPPY FARMER. Robert Schumann	4	3
(Variations from Album for the Young)		
3. THE WILD HORSEMAN. Robert Schumann . . .	7	4
(from Album for the Young)		
4. MILITARY SUITE		
The Marine's Hymn	8	4
The Caisson Song	9	4
Anchors Away	11	5
5. OXFORD GAVOTTE. Susan Kagan	13	6
6. IN THE HALL OF THE MOUNTAIN KING. Edvard Grieg	14	6
(from Peer Gynt)		
7. ASLEEP IN THE DEEP. H. W. Perrie	18	8
8. MARCH OF A MARIONETTE. Charles Gounod	20	9
9. MUSETTE. Johann Sebastian Bach	22	9
10. GAVOTTE. Jean-Baptiste Lully	23	10
11. MARCHE. Wolfgang Amadeus Mozart	25	10
(from Les Petits Riens)		
12. LA VILLAGEOISE. Philippe Rameau	27	11
13. COUNTRY DANCE. Ludwig van Beethoven	28	12
14. HORNPIPE (American Folk Dance)	29	12
15. FALSTAFF'S DRINKING SONG. Otto Nicolai	31	13
(from The Merry Wives of Windsor)		
16. DOWN IN THE DEEP CELLAR. Ludwig Fischer	32	13
17. THE CARNIVAL OF VENICE (Variations) . J. B. Arban	34	14
18. SEVEN DUETS		15

FIRST SOLOS FOR THE TUBA PLAYER

Selected and Arranged by Herbert Wekselblatt

1. Civil War Medley

2. The Happy Farmer

(Variations)

from: Album for the Young

Robert Schumann (1810-1856)

Brisk and lively
Full sound

3. The Wild Horseman

from: Album for the Young

Robert Schumann

4. Military Suite

Anchors Aweigh

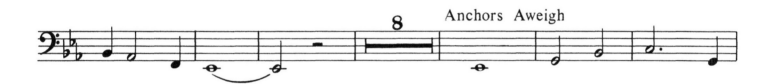

5. Oxford Gavotte

Susan Kagan

6. In the Hall of the Mountain King

from: Peer Gynt

Edvard Grieg (1843-1907)

7. Asleep in the Deep

H. W. Perrie

8. March of a Marionette

Charles Gounod (1818-1893)

9. Musette

Johann Sebastian Bach (1685-1750)

10. Gavotte

Jean-Baptiste Lully (1687)

11. Marche

from: Les Petits Riens

Wolfgang Amadeus Mozart (1756-1791)

12. La Villageoise

Jean Philippe Rameau (1683 - 1764)

13. Country Dance

Ludwig van Beethoven (1770-1827)

14. Hornpipe

American Folk Dance

15. Falstaff's Drinking Song

from: The Merry Wives of Windsor

Otto Nicolai (1810-1849)

16. Down in the Deep Deep Cellar

Ludwig Fischer (1745-1825)

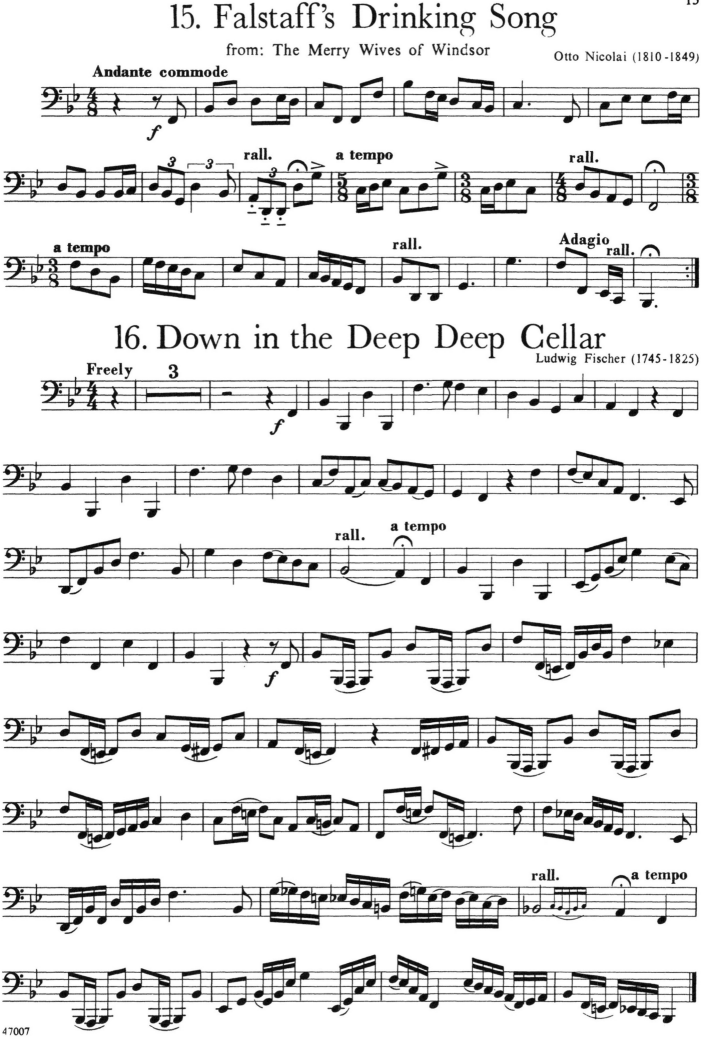

17. The Carnival of Venice

(Variations)

J.B. Arban

18. Seven Duets

1.

Anonymous

Tuba 1 / Tuba 2 — Andante, mf

f

mf

2.

Saint-Jacome

♩. = 76

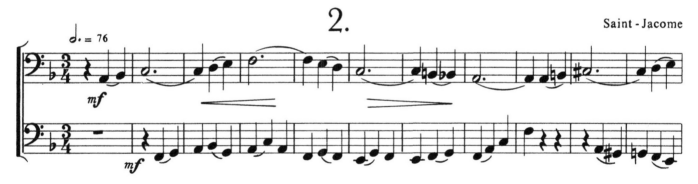

mf / mf

f

rall. a tempo / rall. a tempo

3.

Saint-Jacome

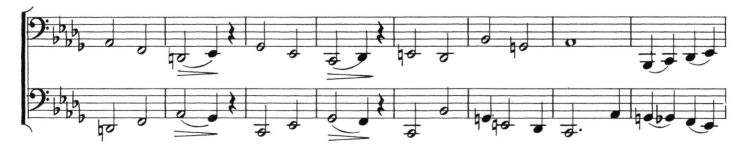

4.

Saint-Jacome

47007

5.

Croft (1678-1727)

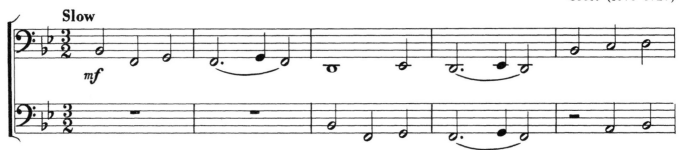

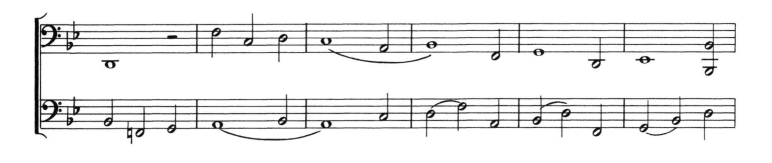

6.
March

Saint-Jacome

47007

7.

P. Müeller

47007

7. Asleep In The Deep

H.W. Perrie

A bit slower

Pause

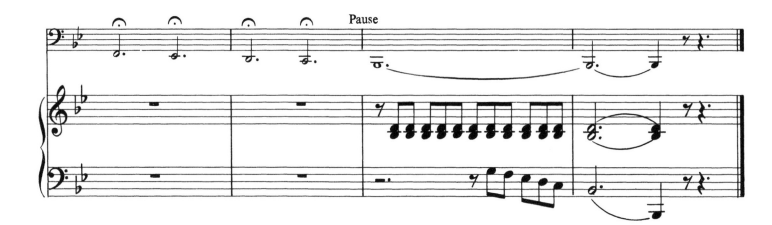

8. March of a Marionette

Charles Gounod (1818-1893)

Allegretto ♩. = 96

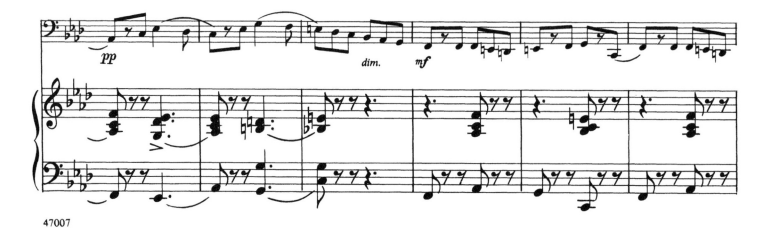

47007

9. Musette

Johann Sebastian Bach (1685–1750)

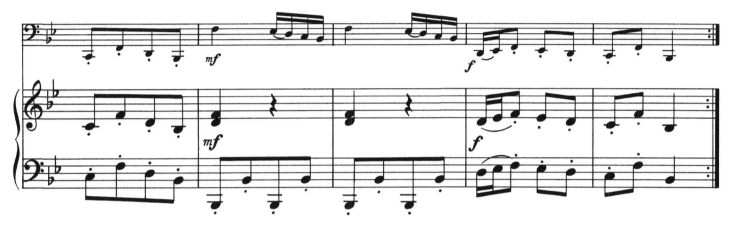

10. Gavotte

Jean-Baptiste Lully (1632-1687)

11. Marche

from: Les Petits Riens

Wolfgang Amadeus Mozart (1756-1791)

47007

12. La Villageoise

Philippe Rameau (1683 - 1764)

47007

13. Country Dance

Ludwig van Beethoven (1770-1827)

14. Hornpipe

American Folk Dance

15. Falstaff's Drinking Song

from: The Merry Wives of Windsor

Otto Nicolai (1810-1849)

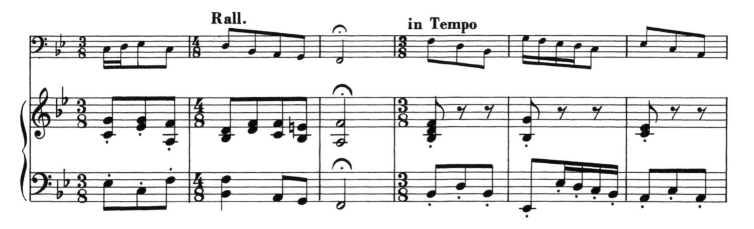

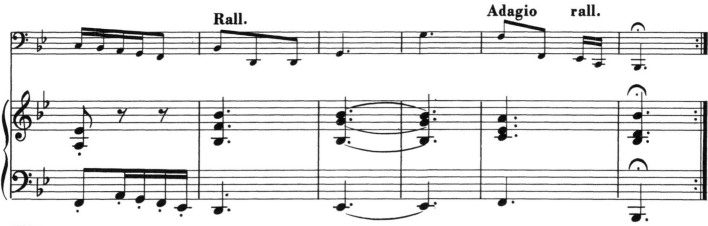

16. Down in the Deep Deep Cellar

Ludwig Fischer (1745-1825)

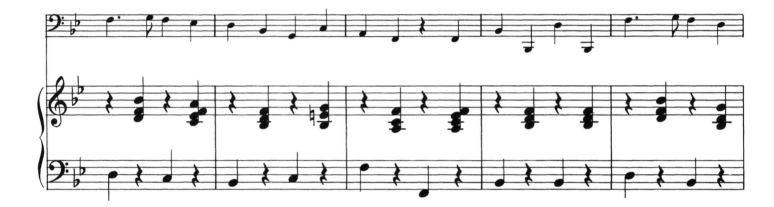

17. The Carnival of Venice

(Variations)

J. B. Arban

47007

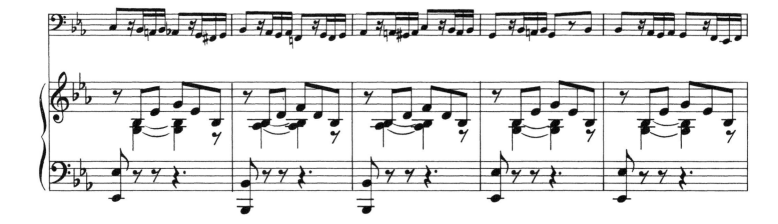